Franc

ois Nepveu, Henry James Coleridge

Of The Love Of Our Lord Jesus Christ, And The Means Of Acquiring

It

Franc

ois Nepveu, Henry James Coleridge

Of The Love Of Our Lord Jesus Christ, And The Means Of Acquiring It

ISBN/EAN: 9783741158537

Manufactured in Europe, USA, Canada, Australia, Japa

Cover: Foto ©Andreas Hilbeck / pixelio.de

Manufactured and distributed by brebook publishing software
(www.brebook.com)

Franc

ois Nepveu, Henry James Coleridge

Of The Love Of Our Lord Jesus Christ, And The Means Of Acquiring

It

OF THE LOVE OF OUR

LORD JESUS CHRIST,

𝔄𝔫𝔡 𝔱𝔥𝔢 𝔐𝔢𝔞𝔫𝔰 𝔬𝔣 𝔞𝔠𝔮𝔲𝔦𝔯𝔦𝔫𝔤 𝔦𝔱.

BY THE REV. FATHER NEPVEU,

OF THE SOCIETY OF JESUS.

The Translation Edited by the Rev. H. J. Coleridge S.J.

LONDON:

BURNS, OATES, & CO., PORTMAN STREET.

———

1869.

PREFACE.

As our LORD JESUS CHRIST was the sole Object of the love of the Eternal Father from all eternity, so ought He to be our only love also. He was sent into the world by the Eternal Father expressly that He might be loved by men. In the New Testament His Father speaks but to commend this love to them. Men are pleasing to Him only so far as they bear resemblance to Jesus Christ. He loves them only inasmuch as they love Jesus Christ. Lastly, He predestines them to eternal glory only by reason of the conformity they have to Jesus Christ.

Jesus Christ Himself came into the world to lead men to this love. All His thoughts,

His desires, His actions, and His sufferings, had this love for their chief aim. He declares that He came into the world for no other purpose than to kindle in the hearts of men the fire of His divine love, and that His chief desire is to see them inflamed with it. " I came to cast fire on the earth, and what will I but that it be kindled ?"—*Ignem veni mittere in terram, et quid volo nisi ut accendatur?*

In all that the Holy Ghost works in our souls, He has no other aim than to teach us to know, love, and imitate our Lord Jesus Christ. Jesus Christ Himself assures us of this, when He says in the Gospel that one of the chief motives of the coming of the Holy Ghost shall be to give testimony of Him to men, and to impress the knowledge of Him on their minds, and the love of Him on their hearts—" When the Paraclete cometh, He shall give testimony of Me."

Lastly, we are Christians only inasmuch as we are united to Jesus Christ. We cannot be perfectly united to Him except by love for Him, and by that entire conformity of our hearts and minds to Him, which this love cannot fail to produce. It is thus only that we are Christians. This love then for Jesus Christ should be the only aim of our desires, the object of our thoughts, the chief occupation of our life, and the end and aim of all our cares and exertions. Sinners may make this, their aim, the imperfect should be always aspiring to it, and the perfect should be unceasingly occupied with it.

What then is the business of our life, if it is not studying, knowing, honouring, loving, and imitating Jesus? This ought to be the chief employment, the chief, or rather, the only devotion of a Christian. Other devotions, I allow, are good; but after all, they are only good in as far as they have reference to this, from which they derive all their merit and all their virtue. This is the solid and essential devotion of Christianity. This it is which makes us true and perfect Christians. Other devotions are often works of supererogation, this is of obligation. Others often oppress us by imposing extra obligations on us, this relieves us by helping us to perform those obligations we already have. Others are means, this is their end. Others assist us towards perfection, this completes and accomplishes our perfection.

Nevertheless, we must own it with sorrow, we see multitudes at this present time in Christendom, who by an intolerable mistake, which we cannot sufficiently deplore, prefer the accessaries to the principal, the means to the end; who entangle themselves in endless devotional practices, and neglect the devotion of devotions, namely, the devotion which we ought to have for the Sacred Person of Jesus Christ. All those, then, who have any zeal for the glory of Jesus Christ should unite in putting an end to such an evil.

This should be the object of the zeal of preachers and the ordinary subject of their sermons; it should be one of the chief cares of those who make a profession of loving Jesus Christ. This is what Directors should aim at above all things, for they should only strive, like St. Paul, to form Jesus Christ in souls; for this is the surest, quickest, and easiest means to conduct souls in a short time to perfection. We may certainly say that many Directors have something to reproach themselves with ·on this score. But this is more especially true of those persons who make a particular profession of devotion, and who even aspire to the highest perfection. For, how is it, that with a number of excellent practices which they observe, with mortifications and austerities, sometimes even excessive, which they undertake, with the assiduous and, as it would seem, elevated prayer to which they apply themselves— how is it that they grovel all their life, scarcely advancing in virtue, sometimes shamefully bending under considerable faults, such as secret pride, and unmortified tempers and passions, so as never to succeed in acquiring to any great degree any of the evangelical virtues, such as deep humility, invariable sweetness, great contempt of the world, complete interior detachment, and a continual mortification of their tempers, senses, and passions? All this comes, doubtless, from not giving their attention sufficiently to the Sacred Person of our Lord Jesus Christ; from not sufficiently studying His Life, His Virtues, His Example, and His Precepts ; from not meditating and penetrating sufficiently His Mysteries, His Greatness, His Merits, His Favours, and the infinite obligations to Him under which we lie ; from not striving to unite themselves constantly to Him by a generous and sincere love, and a perfect conformity of their hearts and minds to Him. It is to attempt to remedy a mistake which has such evil consequences, that Eight Motives are proposed in the First Part of this little work, such as seem the most suitable to inspire us with a great desire to love Jesus Christ and to unite ourselves solely to Him. But as it would be of little use to us to have this desire if we do not put it into practice, Eight Means are provided in the Second Part which may assist us in acquiring this love. In the Eighth of these Means the plan and rules of a holy Association are given, the aim and end of which is to ask continually of the Eternal Father an increase of the love and knowledge of His Son, and perfect conformity of heart and mind with Him.

The blessing which God has already
given to this Means of acquiring love of
Jesus Christ, the approbation of the Holy
Pontiff Innocent XI. of happy memory,
and the Indulgences also which he has
granted to those who become members
of this Association, give hopes that those
who are really devout will be edified by it,
will derive great fruit from so holy an
exercise, and thus see the love and knowledge of Jesus Christ increase.

We may add, that those who aspire to a
perfect union with Jesus Christ, will find in
a separate volume, which is a continuation
of this work, Interior Exercises on all the
Mysteries of the Hidden and Glorious Life
of our Saviour. They may use the book
with profit throughout the whole year,
and thus labour to clothe themselves in
Jesus Christ, and transform themselves
completely in Him.

CONTENTS.

PART THE FIRST

EIGHT MOTIVES EXCITING US TO THE LOVE OF
OUR LORD JESUS CHRIST.

MOTIVE I.

WE SHOULD LOVE JESUS CHRIST, BECAUSE HE IS LOVEABLE.

EVERYTHING that is beautiful, and everything that is perfect, is naturally loveable. Everything that is infinitely beautiful and infinitely perfect, is therefore infinitely and necessarily loveable. Hence it follows that the Blessed, who see clearly the beauty and perfections of God, love Him so necessarily that it is out of their power to refrain from doing so. They would love Him infinitely if they were capable of an infinite love.

Were we then to study more often, were we to know more perfectly Thy perfections, a sweet obligation of loving Thee, since Thou dost contain in Thyself all perfections, created and uncreated, human and divine, spiritual, absolute and relative, and consequently all that can not only satisfy our minds and win our hearts, but even please our affections, and captivate our senses, in a word, all that can attract our love?

Is it not, then, wonderful that in spite of so many reasons for loving Thee, we can possibly avoid doing so? Jesus is God. He possesses, therefore, infinite beauty, infinite goodness, infinite power, holiness, wisdom, and, in a word, every perfection to an infinite degree. Thus, then, my soul, thou canst find in Him wherewith to satisfy thy desires, however vast, however ambitious they may be; wherewith to fill that immense craving of the human heart which cannot be filled with any created or finite good. What then dost thou seek for elsewhere?

But Jesus is also man. In taking a body and a nature like ours, He makes these beauties and perfections of His—all divine as they are—material, sensible, adapted to our weakness, and proportioned to our faculties. How, then, can we refuse to love Jesus, or excuse ourselves from doing so, though we be ever so earthly, material, or attached to the objects of sense? For we have in Jesus, as the object of our love, something which is both divine and human, spiritual and sensible; something which can, consequently, satisfy our minds, our hearts, our reason, and our senses, and attract at the same time our veneration, our love, our admiration, and our tenderness. How comes it, then, that the effect upon us is so often different from this? What are we to think or say of this strange marvel? Only that there is something in the malice of man, and in the insensibility of his heart towards Jesus, as incomprehensible as there is in the goodness and beauty of God.

God became Man, says St. Augustine, in order that man, who is composed of two such different parts, one altogether spiri-

in a God-Man all that was wanting to
make the happiness of both his own natures,
should not be obliged to divide his heart,
and thereby to divide his love, between
God and the creature ; but that, finding in
the Humanity of Jesus a holy occupation
for his affections, pleasure for his senses,
satisfaction for his mind, and enough to
content his heart, he might place all his
joy in Him, and find his happiness in loving
Him. What then! If one touch of beauty,
if the smallest trace of perfection found in
a wretched creature, can dazzle our eyes,
take possession of our minds, and allure our
hearts with a kind of enchantment ; what
strange sort of enchantment is this of
which we speak, that the accumulation of
every beauty and all perfections, divine and
human, spiritual and material, all of which
are found in Thee, most lovely Jesus, is
unable to satisfy our mind, win our heart,
or earn our love? Is it madness? or
blindness? or insensibility? or, rather,
is it not all three at once? For, indeed,
how is it conceivable that, while we can

no more help loving that which is loveable, than help seeing that which is visible, yet Jesus, Who has done everything to make Himself beloved by us, or rather, is Himself alone worthy of love, should be about the only one unloved by us! Unloved! Rather, Who is neglected, scorned, forsaken! It is this pitiable blindness which the Prophet foresaw and deplored in those touching words—" Be astonished, O ye heavens, at this, and ye gates thereof, be very desolate, saith the Lord. For my people have done two evils. They have foresaken Me, the fountain of living water, and have digged to themselves cisterns, broken cisterns, that can hold no water."* This is what happens daily, when we forsake Jesus, infinitely lovely, to run after creatures, the possession of which never contents us, and the love of which, far from making us happy, makes us miserable and even criminal.

This horrible confusion and strange insensibility which no one can comprehend,

and which yet we see every day, touches
to the quick those souls who are penetrated
with the love of our Lord. We ourselves
should bitterly lament it, if we had not
ourselves a share in this insensibility. This
thought, that a God infinitely lovely should
not be loved by men, so inconsolably
afflicted the Saints, such as St. Catharine
of Siena, St. Teresa, and St. Mary Magdalen
de Pazzi, as to to cause them sometimes
to sigh for death, and to cry out in their
holy transports of zeal, love, and suffering :
"Love is not loved, Love is not loved!" Oh,
sons of men ! how long will your minds
be so blinded, and your hearts so weighed
down by earthly things, as to have no
wish to see the One True Beauty, and to
love the One True Love ! Thus it must
be, my sweet and adorable Jesus, till Thou
Thyself, Who art the Light of the World,
shalt so enlighten, elevate, and fortify our
minds as to render them capable of knowing Thee ; until Thou shalt so detach,
purify, and warm our hearts as to render
them capable of loving Thee ; until Thou

shalt not only make known to our minds
Thy Beauty, but also make our hearts
sensible to the power of its charms, so that
we shall confess that there is none but
Thee Who art beautiful, and perfect, and
lovely, and that consequently Thou only
dost deserve our love.

––––––

MOTIVE II.

WE SHOULD LOVE JESUS, BECAUSE HE HAS LOVED US.

LOVE is the only price by which we can
adequately pay for love, and in the same
way also we can say that to love is the
most effectual means of making ourselves
beloved. What limit then should there
be to our love for our Lord Jesus Christ,
Who has loved us as much as it is possible
to love ? He has loved us infinitely more
than we have loved ourselves; and yet to
what length does not our self-love go ?
He has loved us so much, that if all the
Angels and all mankind were to unite and

conspire to love us with all their might,
their love would be less in proportion to
the love of Jesus Christ for us than a drop
of water compared with the ocean. More
than this. Were you to accumulate in
one single heart the love borne to God
through all eternity by all the Saints, by
all the Blessed Spirits, by the Blessed
Virgin herself, all this would not approach
to the love Jesus has for us, because all
such love is finite, but that of Jesus is
infinite. For this reason St. John says,
in speaking of the love of our Lord for
men, that He carried it to an excess. His
love in this instance exhausted His power ;
and though He was God and all powerful,
He put it, as it were, out of His power
to do more for men. " Having loved His
own who were in the world, He loved
them unto the end."* And indeed, if we
consider Christ as God, is it not to have
loved us to excess, never to have been
a single instant from all eternity without
thinking of us, without occupying Himself

about us, without loving us ; and moreover
loving us with a love so efficacious as to
produce in time results so great as we
know ?   If we regard Him as Man, is it
not having loved us to excess, to have
thought of us from the first to the last
moment of His life; not to have made
the slightest movement which was not a
movement of love for us ?   Is it not to
have loved us to excess, to have loved us
more than His repose, more than His glory,
more than His pleasure, more than His
possessions, more than His life, sacrificing
all these that He might win our love ?
Is it not to have loved us to excess, to
have made this sacrifice with joy and
pleasure ?   For His love for us made this
painful sacrifice of Himself sweet and
pleasant to Him, because it was to be
useful to us.   Again, is it not loving us
to excess, to be, as He declared to a Saint,
ready to renew daily this sacrifice for each
one of us, if it were necessary for our salvation and to win our love ?

had for us during His life was such, that had He let its transports go their full length, and not sustained Himself by the power of His Divinity against such intense emotions, the force of His love would have killed Him. What, indeed, would not have been the obligation we should have been under to love Him, had He died from nothing but the excess of His love for us? Do we owe Him less, then, because He miraculously preserved His life against the intensity of His love, that He might sacrifice it for us afterwards by a death equally painful and ignominious? Even then, if Thou, my Divine Lord, wert not in Thyself so lovely as Thou art; if Thou hadst not bestowed such great benefits on us, if Thou hadst not endured such great evils for us, if Thou hadst not delivered us from still greater evils, how could we do less than return Thee love for love?—than love Thee, at least, with all our might, which is finite, since Thou hast loved us with

to refrain from showing love and tenderness
even to an animal if it loves us, or shows
its love by caresses, or appears to have a
special attachment to us ; and yet, the only
love which is uninfluential and powerless
to attract love for love, which rather attracts
scorn and insult, is that of Jesus, which
is eternal, infinite, and disinterested ! Could
there ever be more horrible ingratitude !
Do not let us, my Jesus, be capable of it ;
rather destroy our hearts, which have
hitherto been so sensible to the love of
creatures and so little alive .to Thy love,
than suffer us to live without loving Thee,
as perhaps we have done till now !

For in truth, if Thou wert to ask each
of us, my Jesus, as Thou didst ask St. Peter,
" Lovest thou me ? " * we might be blind
and presumptuous enough to answer as he
did—" Thou knowest, Lord, that I love
Thee." But will not our heart, by its
secret reproaches, belie our words ? For
if we loved Thee, my Divine Saviour,
should we think so little about Thee,

should we occupy ourselves so little with Thee, should we have so little fear of displeasing Thee, so little wish to please Thee? Should we be so little zealous for Thy glory, so little alive to Thy interests, so little affected by the insults daily done unto Thee? Should we have such indifference for Thy inspirations, such infidelity to Thy grace, such ingratitude for Thy benefits, such disregard for Thy maxims, so little zeal in following Thy example? Should we have such horror as we have of those things which Thou didst especially love and embrace—humiliation and suffering—although we know that it is only through them that we are able to resemble Thee, please Thee more, show Thee our love, and merit Thine?

And after all this, shall we dare tell Thee, my Jesus, that we love Thee, without fear of denying the truth and our own conscience, when we consider how little our conduct corresponds to our words? Thou alone, O Lord, canst make my words agree with my conduct, my lips with my heart, by causing me to begin, now at least, to say with truth : " Thou knowest Lord that I love Thee."

MOTIVE III.

WE SHOULD LOVE JESUS, BECAUSE HE ARDENTLY DESIRES WE SHOULD LOVE HIM.

IF we ardently desire the friendship of others, it is either for the gratification we find in it, the advantages we hope to gain from it, the honour it may do us, or the consideration it may obtain for us. None of these motives could influence God in ardently seeking for the friendship of man. Man being in himself so insignificant, his friendship must also be so, especially with regard to God. For, whether we love God or love him not, He is none the less great, or good, or happy, or sufficient for Himself. Nevertheless, says St. Thomas, to see how ardently God desires and seeks the friendship of man, one would say that man was supreme happiness of the Creator depended on the creature, *Quasi homo Dei Deus esset.* One would have thought that we should have considered it a great thing and a special grace, that God should condescend so far as to permit us to love Him. What should we feel then, when Jesus, this God-Man, earnestly desires our love, and begs it eagerly of us ?

The majesty of kings inspires their subjects with such fear and respect as almost to forbid their love, or at any rate, to forbid them the liberty of expressing it ; and a man, unless he is a very privileged favourite, who should think of saying to the king, "I love you," would be set down as either very bold or very foolish. His only reward would be insult, or at least ridicule and scorn. But the Sovereign Majesty of God, before Whom kings are as insignificant as ourselves, is not thus unapproachable. Not only does He permit, He obliges us, to love him, and far from being offended or repelled by our constantly telling Him, "I love Thee, my God," He has a special pleasure, although He knows it before we tell Him, in hearing us often repeat it. David wonders that God should be so willing to remember man. "What is man that thou art mindful of him?"* Job wonders that He should deign look on him. "And dost Thou think it meet to open Thy eyes upon such an one?"† But, according to the opinion of Job, what is beyond all wonder is, that God should care to set His Mind and Heart on loving such a miserable creature. "Why dost Thou set Thy Heart upon him?"‡ Nevertheless, it is this same eagerness and ardour which we find indicated to us in hundreds of places in Scripture. It is indicated in the Book of Proverbs by the earnest cries of un-created Wisdom to attract man to her. "O ye men, to you I call!"§ by that pressing entreaty she makes to man for his heart—"My son, give me thy heart!" It is indicated in the Book of Canticles by the tender anxiety of the Spouse, who

---

* Psalm viii. 5.   ‡ Job vii. 17.
† Job xiv. 3.   § Prov. viii. 4.

typifies Jesus, by that ardour with which
He invites His bride, that is the faithful
soul, to love Him, receive Him, open to
Him the door of her heart, " Open to me,
my sister, my love." * It is indicated in
the Gospel by the ardent zeal with which
the Good Shepherd goes to search for the
lost sheep, by the pain He feels for its loss
and wanderings, by the delight He evinces
on its return. This is what He indicates
on the Cross when saying those words—" I
thirst "†—to show not so much His bodily
thirst, as the ardour with which He desired
the love of men. This is what He again
indicated so plainly by that earnest, thrice
repeated, question He put to St. Peter,
whether he loved Him. Could our Lord
Jesus Christ manifest to us more strongly
than He has done His intense desire that
we should love Him? And yet He is
not satisfied with this. He attracts us by
His benefits—" In all things you are made
rich in Him."‡ He invites us by His
promises—" With Me are riches, that I

* Can. v. 2.   † St. John xix. 28.   ‡ 1 Cor. i. 5.

may enrich those who love Me."* He
urges us by His inspirations—"Behold I
stand at the gate and knock."† He com-
pels us by His commands—"Thou shalt
love the Lord thy God with thy whole
heart."‡ He constrains us, as it were, by
His threats—"He that loveth not, abideth
in death." § In fine, everything He pro-
poses, everything He produces in the order
of nature and of grace, tends only to constrain man to love Him. What then! does
not the reiterated prayer and earnest wish
of some importunate person often force us,
though we care very little about him, to
grant his request ; and shall not the holy
entreaties of Jesus for our love, which is
to cause our happiness, force us to give
it Him ? "Alas," says St. Augustine,
"Thou dost command me, Lord, to love
Thee, and if I refuse, Thou dost threaten
me with the greatest misery. Is there,
then, in the world, any misfortune equal to
that of not loving Thee ? No, my God ;

* Prov. viii. 18, 21.   ‡ Matt. xxii. 37.
† Apoc. iii. 20.   § 1 John iii. 14.

if Thou wishest to frighten me, threaten
me not with the fires of hell, threaten only
that I shall never burn with the fire of
Thy divine love; this threat will be more
terrible to me than a thousand hells. For
if in the flames of hell one spark of Thy
love could fall into the hearts of those
poor reprobate souls, hell would be no
longer hell to them, but a real Paradise.
If, on the contrary, the Blessed could be
in Heaven without loving Thee, Paradise
would no longer be a Paradise to them,
but a real hell."

It seems to me, my Jesus, when I search
my heart, that I really wish, in good faith, to
love Thee. Why is it then that I love Thee
not, though Thou dost desire it, and that
indeed more ardently than I do? Doubtless, it is that my desire is not effectual
or sincere like Thine. Then, my Jesus, it
is for Thee to give me this sincere desire
of loving Thee, or better still, give me
Love itself, for I can never desire Thy
love as I ought, still less acquire it without
Thee!

MOTIVE IV.

WE SHOULD LOVE JESUS, BECAUSE HE HAS OBTAINED FOR AND BESTOWED ON US GREAT BENEFITS.

IT is not without reason that the Apostle tells us that Jesus Christ has enriched us with such prodigalty, that nothing is wanting to us that we can desire—" That in all things you are made rich in Him, so that nothing is wanting to you in any grace."* None but He Who bestowed these benefits on us can perfectly understand their multitude and greatness ; and none but He can make us to comprehend this, at least perfectly. To form in some measure a conception of their multitude, it is sufficient to say, that we owe to Jesus all the blessings of nature, all of grace, and all of glory ; that we owe to Jesus the ineffable benefits of Redemption, Predestination, Election, Justification, and that which is to be seal of all others, Glorification. But let us pause at that of Re-

* 1 Cor. i. 5. 7.

demption, which is the source of all the
others, and which includes in itself so
many others, because Jesus willed to be
our Redeemer. From the first to the last
moment of His life, He thought, and acted,
prayed, and suffered, and laboured, and
lived for us alone. Not a step did He take,
not a word did He utter, not a miracle did
He work, not a sigh did He breathe, not
a tear did He let fall, not a drop of blood
did He shed, which was not for us. So
that we may reckon the benefits conferred
upon us by Jesus, and the obligations we
owe to Him, by every movement of His
Heart and Mind, of which we were always
the object and the end ; by every moment
of His life, for every moment was consecrated to us. Hadst Thou, O Divine
Saviour, bestowed upon us but one sigh,
but one tear, but one throb of Thy Heart,
our obligations to Thee would have been
infinite, since each one of these actions,
coming from an Infinite Being, would have
been of infinite value. What then must
we think and what can we say, but that

we are under, so to speak, an infinity of
infinite obligations to Thee, since Thou
didst not make one movement which was
not for us, and that therefore we have
an infinity of motives for infinitely loving
Thee, were that possible. We owe to Jesus
the favour and friendship of His Father,
the position of children of God and inheritors of eternal happiness. We owe
to Him all the blessings we continue daily
to receive from God. If God preserves us,
protects us, helps us, it is for Jesus' sake.
From Jesus proceed all graces, lights,
inspirations, good thoughts, good dispositions, fidelity to grace, protection from
danger, strength in temptation, constancy
in suffering, patience in adversity, perseverance in good. "In all things you are
made rich in Him." It is, therefore, from
Him, as from our Head, that all these graces
and favours flow down upon us, who are His
members, the smallest of which graces we
cannot obtain but from Him and through
Him. If there is a continual stream, so to
speak, of graces and favours flowing from

the Head to the members, is it not natural there should be a continual reflux of love and gratitude from the members to the Head, from Whom they receive such numberless blessings, and without Whose assistance they can do nothing good? It is this which made the Son of God say, that without Him we can do nothing.* As the branch of the vine cannot bring forth fruit of itself unless it be attached to the stem, so we cannot do good unless we live in Him and in union with Him.

But if these benefits are so important on account of their multitude, much more so are they from the circumstances which accompany them. For there is not one, however insignificant it may appear in itself, which is not in some sort infinite, for it proceeds from an Infinite Being, it springs from an infinite love, and results in an infinite happiness.

There is not one of these benefits which is not eternal. For not only does each proceed from an eternal love, God having

* St. John xv. 5.

generously determined from eternity to bestow this blessing on us, but also because it leads us to eternal happiness. There is not one which is not special to each one of us, however common it may appear. Owing to our self-love and secret pride, which always crave to be preferred before others, we naturally like to be singled out, so that the distinction shown in the graces bestowed on us often affects us more than the graces themselves, which, however great they may be, appear to us to lose part of their merit so soon as they are common to many. But it is not thus with God's benefits, which, though they are common to many, should be looked on as special to each one of us. First, because it is the same with God's favours as with His love, which is undivided and undiminished by the act of communication ; as is the case with the light of the sun, which in illuminating the whole world communicates its light to each one singly with as much fulness as if there were no one else to be illuminated. Secondly, because He gives us graces,

however general and common they may
seem, with as particular an intention as
if there were none but ourselves on whom
to bestow them. Lastly, because His good
will to us is such that He would be
equally ready to bestow His blessings on
us, though there should be none but us to
profit by them. It was this which caused
St. Paul to look on the Redemption with
the same gratitude as he would have felt
had Jesus Christ died for him alone:
" Who loved me, and delivered Himself
for me."*

And not only are the benefits of Jesus
infinite, eternal, and singular, but they are
also continual. His goodness never tires
of doing us good and overwhelming us
incessantly with His graces. We might
count the moments of our lives by the
number of His benefits; and perhaps, by
as many acts of ingratitude on our part.
Again, we are not only indebted to Jesus
for the benefits He bestows on us at this
present time, but also for those He will

bestow on us throughout all eternity, if we are predestinated, as we should hope we are; and not only for these, but also for those He would have bestowed on us had we not frustrated them by our infidelity and resistance—"In all things you are made rich in Him."

If benefits have so wonderful a power in winning hearts, so that even dumb animals cannot refrain from showing love and gratitude to those who are kind to them, what effect should not be made on us by the number of benefits, so many and so vast, which we owe to Jesus? Alas, says William of Paris, what a wonderful miracle is this! a miracle wrought indeed by the power of the devil and not of God, that the heart of man, surrounded with such numberless benefits, like so many burning coals, should remain, in spite of them, a block of ice—*Homo tot congestis carbonibus diabolico miraculo friget ad Deum.*

We pride ourselves on being generous

us by miserable creatures, and alive to feelings of gratitude for benefits which are always of little worth, and often fatal to us. And yet we remain unmoved by the proofs of love shown us by the God-Man! We have no gratitude for benefits which are at the same time both infinite and essential to us!

What! can the benefits of Jesus, which are singular, unceasing, eternal and infinite, and the gifts of a God, can they change their nature? Can they do us harm? Are they alone unworthy of our love, and powerless to excite our gratitude? It is a small thing, indeed, to speak of that they do not win our gratitude—but that we should repay them with indifference and coldness, and the blackest of all ingratitude, can we think of this without astonishment? Can we own ourselves guilty without dying of shame or grief?

As a climax to Thy graces, my amiable Jesus, Thou must add one other, without which they will not only be useless but fatal to me. It is to impress on my heart, a sincere and tender gratitude for these benefits, and a constant, generous love of Thee, Who art the Author of them. This, as a crown to all the others, is the great and, henceforth, the only favour which, through Thyself, I ask of Thee.

MOTIVE V.

WE SHOULD LOVE JESUS, BECAUSE HE HAS GIVEN HIMSELF TO US.

WHATEVER may have been the blessings or the gifts of our Lord to man, they were insufficient fully to satisfy the desire which God had to communicate Himself infinitely. Nor were they sufficient to satisfy the capacity man had of receiving more, and thus his heart, still feeling empty in the midst of this abundance, cried out, lamenting with a Saint—"Whatever Thou givest me, will never satisfy me, so long as Thou givest me not Thyself!" It was therefore requisite that Jesus, after having self — *Non jam sua, sed seipsum nobis impendit.*

This He accomplished in instituting the Sacrament of the Eucharist, in which He gives Himself wholly to us, that is His Body, His Blood, His Soul and all the merits of that Holy Soul, His Divinity and all the perfections of that Divinity ; and all this He has given in the most perfect manner possible.

The perfection of a gift depends on three things : that we should have it in our own immediate possession, have absolute control and have entire use of it. These three things are amply found in the gift which Jesus makes of Himself to us in the Holy Eucharist.

(1.) The possession of it is as intimate and as immediate as it is possible to be. For it is not accomplished only by union of will, harmony of mind, and conformity of affections and sentiments, but by an intimate union of the Real and Physical Body of Jesus Christ with the body and soul of him who receives It.

(2.) The dominion which we acquire over
the body of Jesus Christ is absolute. We
are able to do what we please with Him,
absolutely and unreservedly. We can retain
Him in our churches, carry Him through
our streets, take Him into our houses,
visit Him, touch Him, receive Him, feed
on Him, consume Him, and, which is still
more astonishing, He yields Himself unreservedly into the power even of the
greatest wretches, though He knows well
they will only use their power to insult
and profane Him! What, in the whole
world, is there over which we have such
absolute power?

(3.) The use of it is entire. Jesus Christ
is everything to us in the Eucharist. In
His Incarnation He made Himself our
Brother; in His Birth, our Companion;
in His Life, our Model; in His Doctrine,
our Master; in His Death, our Redeemer;
in His Glory, our Recompenser. Jesus
is all these at once to us in the Eucharist.
Let us rather say He is more to us in
It than this: for He is also our Father,

our Brother, our Master, our Companion,
our Food, our Pastor, our Medicine, our
Physician, our Viaticum, our Guide, the
Price of our ransom, our Redeemer, our
Reward, our Recompenser. Cannot I truly
say, then, as St. Bernard did, that Jesus
in the Eucharist has given Himself wholly
to me, He is occupied wholly for me, and
He has consecrated Himself wholly to my
wants—*Totus mihi datus, totus in meos
usus expensus.*

Surely, then, if Jesus has given Himself
wholly to us, we cannot refuse to give ourselves wholly to Him.   He fruitlessly
exhausted the treasures of His liberality,
the might of His power, and the attractions
of His love, to win our hearts ; and seeing
that do what He would, and give what
He would, He could not make us love
Him, He at last gave us Himself, that He
might merit our love. After having resisted
all His gifts and all His graces, can we
hold out against Himself ? If there had
been anything better than Himself to give
us, He would have given it. But though

He is God, He is powerless to give us anything better than Himself—*Quid enim poterat dare melius seipso !* (St. Bernard).

Alas, said St. Bernard, if I am incapable of acknowledging all the blessings Thou hast bestowed on me, how shall I be able to acknowledge the benefit by which Thou givest me Thyself? If Thou wert to demand of us all our goods, our blood, our life, should we sufficiently repay Thee for what Thou givest us, when Thou givest us Thy Own Self in the Eucharist ? Should we be giving Thee anything which equalled the value of a God ? But Jesus does not demand as much as this of us. He simply asks for a little love ; a little of that love which we lavish so unworthily on creatures, and which we refuse only to Jesus, Who alone is worthy of it. We love a slave or a dumb animal because it is ours ; and yet, Thou, my Jesus, we love Thee not, though Thou art all our own, and though Thou hast made Thyself all ours in a way so capable of winning us to love Thee !

Thou thinkest not that it is giving me

too much to give me Thy whole Self.
And yet I hesitate whether to give myself
wholly to Thee! Is it then, my soul, such
a great misfortune to belong wholly to
thy Jesus, that thou shouldst hesitate so
long before thou canst resolve upon it?
Alas, my Saviour, I have often told Thee
that I gave Thee my heart, and that I
wished to be all Thine, but either I was
insincere and false in my words, or else
I have been inconstant in my resolutions.
But now, my Divine Jesus, I wish to be
really, unreservedly, and for ever Thine.
Therefore I give Thee the irrevocable gift
of my heart. I consecrate to Thee my
body and soul, all the thoughts of my
mind, all the emotions of my heart, and
all the actions of my life. I renounce
henceforth all motions contrary to this
gift which may escape me through frailty
or unwariness, and I protest that I will be
all Thine in life and in death, in time and
eternity. Every good thing is yours, said
St. Paul, to the Faithful, because Jesus
Christ has obtained all goods for you; as for

you, ye are Christ's. What riches! What
happiness! Too happy if we possess them,
happier still, if Jesus possesses us!

MOTIVE VI.

WE SHOULD LOVE JESUS, BECAUSE HE HAS SUFFERED MUCH FOR US.

THERE is no stronger, no more convincing
proof of love than to suffer for one we love.
In comparison with this, all others are
either doubtful, or at any rate trifling.
Benefits are, I allow, strong and tangible
proofs of friendship, but after all, we only
show in giving our goods that we prefer
our friends to our goods, of which we
deprive ourselves so willingly for their
sakes; but in suffering for them, we prove
that we prefer them to ourselves. It was
then, in this way, that the Son of God
desired, at whatever cost, to convince us
of the strength and greatness of His love,
in order that He might thereby merit ours.
Though He had done so much for us, and

given Himself to us, He still considered
it insufficient, either to satisfy His love or
to merit ours, until He had convinced us
of it by submitting Himself for our sakes
to the severest sufferings, the most horrible
tortures, and the most cruel and ignominious of deaths. But if His sufferings
provide us with such strong motives for
loving Him, much more so do they from
the circumstances which accompany them,
for there it not one of these which is not
in itself a motive for loving Him.

It is a God Who suffers; therefore no
extraneous power can constrain Him, since
being God, He is independent. Being the
Holy of Holies, He had no faults to expiate
and no pain to suffer on His own part,
therefore there was nothing to oblige Him.
Neither on our side was there any reason
which could compel Him ; for not only were
we poor vile creatures, but His rebellious
and ungrateful enemies. Had we been all
annihilated or damned, He would have
been none the less great and none the less
happy. And yet, that He might deliver

us from everlasting torments, which we deserved, and to obtain for us everlasting happiness, which we could not deserve, He exposed Himself to suffering for our ransom, as if our misery were His, or as if the preservation of His Being and His greatest happiness depended on ours. Any one forming a clear conception of what God is and what man is, the greatness of the one and the meaness of the other, would find it hard to make these two extremes meet—a God dying for man. But should he be happy enough to conceive this, I mean a God forgetting Himself and His greatness so far as to die for man, he would find enough to occupy the rest of his life in wonder and admiration, even to die of grief or love at the thought of it. It was this that forced a Saint to exclaim in an ecstacy of love and astonishment : "What! do I see my Love dying on the Cross, and yet I can live"—*Amor meus crucifixus est, et ego vivo.* But if I do live, let it be on condition that I live henceforth for Jesus only, Who so willingly died for me—"That they also who live, may not now live to themselves but unto Him Who died for them."*

In the second place, what makes this still more admirable is, that our Lord, had He willed, could have ransomed us by one drop of His Blood, by one tear, by one sigh, or by the least movement of His Heart, because there could be no action performed by this God-Man which was not of infinite value, proceeding as it did from One of infinite dignity. And yet, instead of this, my adorable Jesus, for our ransom Thou didst choose to suffer the fiercest persecutions, the blackest calumnies, the most merciless outrages and insults, the most cruel tortures, and at last, after having poured out Thy Blood to its very last drop, to die in the extreme of agony and obliquy on the Cross, in order to prove to us the excess of Thy love by the excess of Thy sufferings, and also that we, seeing what we had cost Thee, might be unable to refuse to give ourselves up wholly to

Thee. *Redemit undâ cùm posset guttâ"*
(St. Bernard).

Thirdly. If the love of Jesus Christ is
proved to us by what He suffered, still better
is it proved by the ardour and eagerness
with which He desires to suffer—" With
desire I have desired," He says Himself, "to
eat this Pasch with you before I suffer."*
"And I have a baptism wherewith I am
to be baptised : and how am I straitened
until it be accomplished !"† He treats His
most zealous disciple as Satan, because He
would have opposed His intention of dying
for men. Again, on the Cross, He shows
His impatience to suffer by saying that He
still thirsts ; for His thirst to suffer for
man's salvation is not appeased by the
out-pouring of all His Blood. If, when
in the Garden of Olives, He showed a
dread of suffering, and asked that He might
not drink of the Chalice of His Passion,
far from making us less grateful, this should
but increase our gratitude to Him. For if
He abandoned Himself voluntarily to the

* St. Luke xxii. 15.　　　*Ibid.,* xii. 50.

weakness of our nature, it was that His sufferings might be more intense, and so might cost Him more, and prove to us more plainly the greatness of His love.

Fourthly. Our loving Saviour was not contented with an ardent desire alone of the sufferings of His Passion. By a wonderful invention of His love, He found a means of anticipating them, and of foretasting the cruelty of His executioners, by permitting His Heart, in His Agony, to suffer a martyrdom a thousand times more cruel than that which He suffered in His Sacred Body at the hands of His persecutors.

Fifthly. He suffered all these tortures without the slightest alleviation. He did not use the power of His Divinity to comfort, but simply to sustain Himself, so that by supporting His life, which would naturally have sunk at once under the weight of His sufferings, He might be able to lengthen the time of His sufferings for us. If He had any consolation, it was only in the thought that it was for us He suffered ; that His sufferings would be useful to us ;

and that perhaps they would soften the
hardness of our hearts and make us love
Him.   It was to such an extent as this
that Jesus in His Passion was carried by
His love for men ; this forced Him to cry
out when He was dying : " It is consum-
mated."*   His sufferings and His love
could go no further—God as He was, He
was powerless to do more for men.

Lastly, what makes all these circumstances of the Passion of our Lord still
more admirable is, that He does not
demand of us, as a proof of our gratitude
for all He suffered, a sacrifice of our goods,
or our repose, our pleasures, our honour, or
our life.   And yet has He not the right
to ask this of us ?   Could we, without ingratitude and injustice, refuse this to Him ?
He demands nothing of us but our love
as His only reward, and as our only proof
of gratitude to Him.   As to the manner
of showing our love, He asks nothing but
that we should not offend Him.   And after
all this, as if He were too well repaid for

* St. John xix. 30.

His sufferings, and as if He yet owed us
something, He promises us eternal happiness on condition that we do not offend
Him. What condescension ! What love !
What goodness !

Truly, can we think of all these circumstances of the Passion of God, in which
His love shines out so clearly, without
being touched and penetrated to our very
heart ? Must we not be more unfeeling
than the wild beasts, harder than the rocks,
if we remain unmoved by the love of a
God dying from the excess of His love for
us, and if we cannot give Him love for love?

If a man or a slave, or the lowest of all
creatures, had endured but the hundredth
part of what Jesus endured for us, although
under very different circumstances, we could
not have refrained from loving him, being
grateful to him, or at least showing signs
of compassion and sorrow for his sufferings,
and saying sometimes with a sigh : " After
all, this poor wretch loved me ; had he not
loved me he would not have suffered as
much." Yet the love shown by a God,

dying on a Cross, or rather, dying more from the intensity of His love than from what He suffered, is the only proof of love to which we remain unmoved, which we repay with coldness and indifference! Is it possible to believe that rational men, men with hearts, should be capable of such gross ingratitude, such strange hardness, to which, except with regard to God, we can find no parallel?

I freely avow, that in the difficulty we naturally have in submitting our understanding to what Faith teaches us about the eternity of the pains of hell, nothing helps me better to understand it than the conduct of the greater number of Christians—their indifference, or rather their ingratitude, and the readiness with which they constantly offend a God and Saviour Who so loved them as to die on a Cross for them. Is it possible that hell, or even a thousand hells, could adequately expiate the frightful insensibility and continual ingratitude of men, who do not love the God-Man, Jesus, Who was crucified for them? Who do not

love Him, did I say?—rather, who despise
Him more shamefully than they would
despise the most abject creature, and who
insult him more cruelly than they would
insult their most implacable enemy!

Ah! my Saviour, now I understand why
it is that in the great Day of Thy Ven-
geance Thou wilt show Thy Cross in the
Heavens. No doubt the sight of the Cross
will be more terrible to reprobate Christians
than the sight of the exterminating angels,
or the devils, or the fire of hell, or even
the sight of Thy angry countenance, for
it will remind them of the excess of Thy
love, and the excess of their ingratitude
towards a Saviour fastened to that Cross,
and expiring for them thereon. Yes! who-
ever well understands those almost incomprehensible words, *A God crucified for men,*
will not find it hard to understand those
others, however incomprehensible they may
sound,—*The same ungrateful men punished
by God with eternal torment.* Grant, my
Jesus, that I may understand them so well
in this life, that in the next I may not

be so unfortunate as to understand and feel them by bitter experience! For indeed, my Saviour, if we love Thee not, we bear witness to our own condemnation, and we must admit that all those who would not burn in this life with the flames which Thy goodness and mercy have sought to kindle in their hearts, deserve to burn in the flames which Thy anger and Thy justice have kindled in hell.

MOTIVE VII.

WE SHOULD LOVE JESUS, BECAUSE OF THE RELATION IN WHICH HE STANDS TO US.

WE cannot help loving those who have some connection with us. It is like a secret though powerful charm which sweetly attracts our hearts, or like an invisible chain which almost imperceptibly draws us together. The same reason which imposes on us the pleasant necessity of loving ourselves obliges us almost as necessarily to love, and with a tender love, those with whom we are connected, as if they were our second selves, or at least part of ourselves.

This is why Jesus, Who desired to win, not only our love, but our tenderest affection, chose to stand towards us in every relation that could help to excite this love in us. We will not speak of our relation to Jesus as our God, our Creator, our King, or our Master, for these titles create in us feelings as much of awe and fear as of love and tenderness. He is our Saviour, for He has delivered us from sin and its fatal consequences, that is from the slavery of the devil, the hatred and anger of His Father, and eternal death. And that we might understand the full virtue of His merits and the plenteousness of His redemption, He was not satisfied with only delivering us from these evils, but He obtained for us those opposite blessings of liberty, of grace, the friendship of His Father, and the position of children of God, and inheritors of eternal life: "Thou shalt call His Name

JESUS, for He shall save His people from their sins."*

He is our Father, for He conceived us on the Cross in the intensity of His sufferings and in the ardour of His love. He gave us birth to the life of grace, through that Wound which opened His Side and pierced His Heart — "Is not He thy Father, that hath made thee, and created thee?"†

He is our Brother, not only because He has made Himself resemble us in nature, when He made Himself Man like us, but also because He has chosen us for His brethren by a kind of adoption, and made us joint-heirs with Himself. St. Paul also tells us that He was not ashamed to call us His brothers.‡

He is the true Spouse of our souls, as He says Himself: "Behold the Bridegroom cometh;"§ but a Spouse of Blood, for this alliance with us has cost Him all His Blood; a Spouse, Who gives to His

---

* St. Matt. i. 21.   ‡ Heb. ii. 11.

Brides, for their dowry, nothing less than Eternal Life; a Spouse, Whose love makes us chaste, Whose holy embraces purify us, as said that generous Virgin and illustrious Martyr St. Agnes; and Who makes us, by the union we have with Him, completely happy and perfectly holy.

He is our Shepherd, Who not only leads and protects His sheep, but also feeds them with His own Body and Blood, after having exposed and given His life for them—" I am the Good Shepherd."*

He is our Physician, for He came down on earth only to heal us of our diseases; and He assures us that it was not for the healthy, but for the sick, that He came.† Nay more, He is that wonderful Physician Who makes a salve of His own Blood to heal our wounds.

Lastly, He is our faithful and constant Friend. For though He is God, He does not disdain to take to Himself this title, and He seems even to take pride in it—" I will not now call you servants, but I have

* St. John x. 11.   † St. Matt. ix. 12.

called you friends."* This is all the more wonderful, since we see amongst men, that kings give willingly enough the name of favourites to their subjects, but would think it derogatory to their dignity to call them friends.

Well then, should not all these our relations to Jesus attract our love and excite our tenderness? Can a poor wretch help loving His Liberator and Saviour? Can a son help loving his Father, and the best of Fathers? *Nemo tam Pater*—" No one is so much a Father as God ;" or a bride her Spouse — a Spouse to Whom she owes everything? Can a brother help loving the most amiable of Brothers, Who comes not to lessen his possessions by taking His own part of them, but to impart to him all His own possessions, which are infinite? Can a sheep not love the Shepherd Who preserves its life by giving His own for its? Can a sick man fail to love the Physician Who cures him by making a remedy of His own Blood? or a friend,

to love the tenderest and most generous
of Friends ?   Ah ! if a single one of these
claims, a single one of these relations
is so powerful amongst men to excite
their affection ; if by these means extra-
ordinary impressions are made and wonderful effects are produced every day on
their hearts, what impressions, my Divine
Jesus, ought not to be made on us by all
these relations united in Thee, which are
far more real than any we can have with
a creature ?   Do they not oblige us to con-
centrate all our affections on Thee ?   In
Thee alone do we find all the qualities
and all the motives capable of exciting
our tenderness and attracting our love.
We ought therefore no longer to divide our
hearts so unworthily ; but, in future, love
nothing but Jesus, or at any rate, nothing
but in Jesus, and through Jesus.

MOTIVE VIII.

WE SHOULD LOVE JESUS, BECAUSE ALL OUR HAPPINESS AND PERFECTION CONSIST IN LOVING HIM.

IF we are not generous enough to love Jesus out of gratitude, let us at least be wise enough to love Him from self-interest. If the blessings we receive from Him cannot move us, let us at least be moved by those we hope to receive. Ah! what blessings may we not hope to receive from Him! If we are so senseless as not to love Jesus for His own sake, we ought, at any rate, to be self-interested enough to love Him for our own. We find in the love of Jesus our own sweetness and our repose. Our perfection is bound up in it ; and our happiness in time and eternity depends on it.

(1.) We find in this our delight and repose. If Jesus was made for us, so also we are made for Jesus. Our hearts therefore can never be satisfied, nor our minds at rest, without possessing Jesus. Now,

we possess Him by loving Him.   Other
things may occupy our hearts and interest
our minds, but they can never perfectly
satisfy either of them.   It is only the love
of Jesus that can make us taste real sweetness.   Those who love Jesus know well
by their own . experience the infinite
sweetness, the solid consolations, the holy
delights which they taste in the practice
of this sacred love, and which are sometimes so intense that the infirmity of
human nature cannot support them, and
is constrained to beg of Jesus either to
strengthen its weakness, or to moderate
His favours.   But we must love if we
would experience these things ; and we
must experience them before we can understand, or even believe in them.

We are fain to taste of this sweetness,
but we wish it to cost us nothing.   For, in
truth, nothing is so pleasant as to love,
especially to love one like Jesus.   There
is no one who would not acknowledge this ;
and no one, I imagine, who does not desire
it.   But there is no way to this love

except through death; none to the sweetness
of the one except through the bitterness
of the other: and this road few care to
follow. We are very willing to accompany
Jesus with His disciples to Mount Thabor,
but we forsake Him on Calvary as they
did. We wish to participate in the highest
favours of Jesus and share at the same
time those of the world; to possess the
delights of Heaven without losing those of
earth; and to taste the purest spiritual
pleasures without renouncing the pleasures
of sense. And yet this cannot be. O my
Divine Jesus, since we cannot live without
pleasure, adapt Thyself to our weakness,
and give us a foretaste of Thy joys, that
we may quit without difficulty those of
the world! Give us a little of that living
water which Thou didst offer to the Sama-
ritan woman. Pour, along with Thy grace
into our hearts, a drop of that celestial dew,
that holy unction, which may enable us to
taste how sweet Thou art, O Lord, and fill
us with a distaste for creatures, which will
make us regard, not only with disdain

but even with horror, all the fatal pleasures
of the flesh, and all the false sweetness
of the world !

(2.) Our perfection is bound up in this,
not only because it consists in this love,
and, as St. Augustine says, the beginning
of perfection is the beginning of love—not
because the growth of one is the growth of
the other, and perfect love is the consum-
mation of perfection—but because it may
well be said that this love is a means of
attaining perfection, and that the surest,
easiest, and quickest road to gain perfection
in a short time, is to endeavour from the
first to love the Sacred Person of our Lord
Jesus Christ, and to apply ourselves with
all our might to acquire His love. For
this love, even when in its beginning, and
as yet imperfect, generally inspires even
sensible devotion, and makes it easy to
overcome a thousand obstacles that often
alarm and even arrest the steps of those
who are beginning to walk in the way of
perfection. Would to God that Directors
made greater use of this method ! they

would assuredly draw great fruit from it.

It is this love alone that can sweeten those virtues which seem to us so austere and so opposed to our passions, so contrary even to our reason, so painful to our senses, and in which notwithstanding Evangelical Perfection consists—I mean the hatred of ourselves, the constant renunciation of our natural inclinations, and the love of crosses and humiliations. In inducing us to love Jesus, as being so worthy of our love, it accustoms us to look, at first without aversion, and afterwards even with love, upon those virtues which Jesus so deeply loved, and of which He gave us such beautiful examples ; which we cannot indeed love except upon those grounds, but which cannot fail of being loved by every soul that sincerely loves Jesus.

In fact, if love either supposes or naturally creates a resemblance between the loved and the lover, we cannot love Jesus without earnestly desiring to resemble Him,

and placing in that resemblance our greatest
happiness. We cannot be like Him unless
we have the same sentiments, the same
inclinations, and the same affections; and
we cannot have these if we do not value,
do not love, do not embrace that which
He valued, and loved, and embraced;
namely, those sufferings, poverty, and humiliations, which were both in His life and
in His death, such dear and inseparable
companions of Jesus Christ. We cannot,
then, love Jesus, nor prove to Him our love,
unless we love poverty, sufferings, and
humiliations. Is there anything in this
argument which is not either of faith or
self-evident? And if it is thus, how many
are there even among Christians, even
among those who make a profession of
devotion, who really love Jesus? Let us,
who read this, search our own hearts on
this point, and without deceiving ourselves
think it over seriously in the presence of
God, and at the foot of the crucifix.

Alas my Jesus! with what shame does
this examination fill me! how frightened I

am at this consideration, for it proves clearly
to me that I love Thee not! And what
am I doing, or what am I, if I do not love
Thee? Either a Christian but in name,
or an actual reprobate! Ah, my Saviour!
let me begin by what is easiest, namely,
by loving Thee, in order that I may afterwards do that which is more difficult, and
love that which alone Thou didst love—
poverty, suffering, and humiliation.

(3.) Our Happiness in Time and Eternity depends on the love of Jesus Christ.
For this is the surest means of deserving
the love of His Eternal Father, Who loves
us only in as much as we love His Son,
as Jesus has Himself told us—"For the
Father Himself loveth you, because you
have loved Me."* He gives us graces out
of consideration for Jesus alone, and according to our devotion to Him. He has
made our eternal happiness depend on our
conformity to Him—"For whom He fore-
knew He also predestinated to be made
conformable to the image of His Son."†

---

* St. John xvi. 27. † Rom. viii. 29.

Thus we may say that love for the Sacred
Person of our Lord Jesus Christ, is at
the same time the most efficacious cause,
the most visible proof, and the surest
pledge of our predestination. In conclu-
sion, then, let us love Jesus if we love
ourselves. Let us love Him at least from
self-interest, if we are not sufficiently just
to love Him from a sense of what is due
to Him, nor disinterested enough to love
Him out of a pure generosity. Woe to
us if we live, but still greater woe if we
die, without having loved Jesus. St. Paul
pronounced an anathema for time and
eternity against those who love not our
Lord Jesus Christ.* But why pronounce
it against such poor wretches? Do not
they themselves pronounce it against themselves by wilfully separating themselves
from Jesus? For can there be a more
terrible excommunication than such a se-
paration? And are they not separated from
Him when they are not united to Him?
And do they not cease to be united to

* 1 Cor. xvi. 22.

Him as soon as they do not love Him? Ah my Jesus! I consent to be banished from the hearts and minds of all men, to be shut out from all communication with creatures, deprived of all the pleasures and good things of this life, on condition that I am not banished from Thy Heart, and that I am not in any way separated from Thee! What evil have I not to dread when I am without Thee? Without Thee, I should despise the delights of Paradise; with Thee, I should not fear the flames of hell.

PART THE SECOND.

———

MEANS I.

OFTEN TO ASK FOR THIS LOVE.

THE first means of acquiring the love of our Lord Jesus Christ is to ask God for it often, or rather, continually. If we had a real desire of loving Jesus Christ, we should use scarcely any other prayer than this, which is by itself sufficient to make us perfect and happy. Thus some devout persons make every day three visits to the Blessed Sacrament, for this intention.

The first, in honour of the Eternal Father, to beg that He, Who so greatly desires us to love His Son, and Who sent Him into the world expressly for that purpose, will teach us Himself how to love Him.

The second, in honour of the Son, to beg Him to kindle in our hearts that holy fire which He tells us He came to bring into the world, and with which He so passionately desires to inflame our hearts.

The third, in honour of the Holy Ghost, praying Him that, since our Lord Jesus Christ has promised to send us this Spirit to give testimony of Him,* He will make this testimony so present and efficacious on our minds and hearts, that so we may receive a perfect knowledge of Jesus, and so may learn to love Him perfectly. Those who wish to practise so easy and effectual a means, can make use of the three prayers to the Three Persons of the Blessed Trinity, which we have composed expressly for this purpose, and which will be found at the end of this book.

* St. John xv. 26.

MEANS II.

TO MEDITATE FREQUENTLY ON THE PERFECTIONS OF OUR LORD JESUS CHRIST, AND ON HIS BENEFITS TO US.

THE second means is to meditate often on the Greatness, Perfections, Mysteries, Maxims, Examples, in short, on all the actions and words of our Lord Jesus Christ. These should be nearly the only subjects of our meditation. It is, as Saint Teresa remarks, a dangerous mistake into which some Directors and some devout people fall, in an age too in which a tendency to over refinement prevails, when they suppose that the Sacred Person of our Lord Jesus Christ is not an object sufficiently elevated for the contemplation of some souls; as if there could be anything greater or more exalted than a Man-God. We should endeavour, for this purpose, to form a high conception of our Lord, to obtain as far as we are able the most perfect knowledge of Him. We should take for our general reading such

books as have best treated of Him, and
which can give us the highest conception
of Him, such as the Gospels, especially
that St. John; St. Paul's Epistles; the
Life of St. Teresa, written by herself; the
works of that great servant of God, that
man so full of the Spirit of Jesus Christ,
Father Avila; the Glories of Jesus, by
Cardinal Berulle; the first two books of
the Knowledge of and Love of our Lord,
by Father St. Jure; the Practice of the
Love of God, by Father Huby; The Interior Christian; and many other works
written on this subject with so much knowledge and unction.

MEANS III.

TO GO TO HOLY COMMUNION FOR THIS INTENTION.

THE third, and undoubtedly the most
efficacious means of acquiring the love of
our Lord Jesus Christ is often to approach

by frequent and devout Communions. I say by frequent Communions; for those who really wish to love Jesus Christ, since they ought to be detached from the world, or to have at least a sincere desire to be detached from it, should not go to Holy Communion more rarely than once a week, and should moreover endeavour to make themselves worthy of going more frequently. For there is no better way of showing their desire of loving Jesus, than by the ardent wish to use this most efficacious means of acquiring His love.

For, in the first place, the Blessed Sacrament is like a furnace of love, which we cannot ever approach in the right dispositions without being fully penetrated and inflamed with this Divine Fire, "like lions breathing forth flame," as St. Chrysostom says. Jesus in the Blessed Sacrament is in fact, at the same time, the Cause, the Object, and the Motive of this love—a Cause most efficacious, an Object most powerful, and a Motive most stringent.

Adorable Sacrament, the chief design of our Lord in coming into our hearts was to produce in them His love, as He testifies Himself by those words: "He that eateth My Flesh and drinketh My Blood, abideth in Me and I in him"*—that is, unites himself with Me by a very close union, and a very intimate love. "As I live by the Father," He says in another place, "so he that eateth Me the same also shall live by Me."†

Can we think that our Saviour will deceive us, or that He will be unfaithful in fulfilling His promises, if we on our part are faithful in bringing with us the requisite dispositions? Let us, then, go often to Holy Communion with an ardent desire, as well as with a perfect confidence, of obtaining a tender and sincere love for our Lord Jesus Christ. Let us be assured that He will infallibly kindle in our hearts that divine Fire, which He came from Heaven to bring to us, and with which He desires to inflame the whole world.

And we may say that the Eucharist is like
a sacred hearth, where He preserves and
cherishes this holy Fire till the consum-
mation of all things, and that it is impos-
sible to approach It, if we have the requisite
dispositions, without being inflamed, or at
least warmed by It—"I am come to cast
fire upon the earth, and what will I but
that it be kindled!"*   We may say that if
God is "a consuming Fire,"† as He is called
in Scripture, it is most especially in the
Blessed Sacrament that He deserves this
title, and in It that He produces these
results.   And as we see that the sun, when
its rays are collected and made more
powerful by being concentrated in a mirror,
acquires a more intense glow and has more
force to burn up objects: so Jesus Christ
by gathering together in the Eucharist
all the ardour of His love, and bringing
it home to us in the Sacramental Species,
makes it, as it would seem, more intense
and more able to kindle His love in our
hearts, which, cold as they may appear

can scarce resist its heat—"There is no one that can hide himself from His heat."*

<hr/>

MEANS IV.

TO HAVE JESUS CHRIST ALWAYS PRESENT.

THE fourth means of easily acquiring this love is to accustom ourselves to have our Lord Jesus Christ as much as possible always present to us. This may be done in three ways.

(1.) When we are about to do any action, we can represent to ourselves the manner in which Jesus Christ did it when on earth, the spirit with which He animated it, and the intention by which He elevated even those acts which seem the very lowest; and thus we can conform ourselves to them, and perform our action in a spirit of union with His.

(2.) By thinking of Him in Heaven, whence He ever looks down upon us, and pours forth incessantly His graces and favours over us, and inspires us with all the good emotions we have within us, being Himself the Head and we the members. Thus, there is no blessing, no grace, no good inspiration which we receive but from Him and by Him.

(3.) By accustoming ourselves to see the Person of our Lord Jesus Christ in our neighbour, as He commands us Himself, assuring us that what we do for our neighbour we do for Him.

Thus, servants in the person of their masters, children in the person of their parents, and wives in the person of their husbands should see Jesus Christ alone. And this is a practice from which many benefits flow.

For first, it cannot be carried out without their thinking often of the Person of our Lord Jesus Christ.

Secondly, they will merit as much as if they had performed the service for Jesus Christ Himself.

actions with much greater facility and perfection.

Fourthly, they will avoid many mis-
takes, and annoyances, and outbursts of
temper into which we fall from want of
due attention to ourselves as well as to
our Lord. This would not happen if we
accustomed ourselves to see Him in the
person with whom we are dealing.

MEANS V.

TO SPEAK OFTEN OF OUR LORD.

THE fifth means is to have a few pious
and intimate friends with whom we can
converse frequently of the greatness and
the perfections of our Lord, and the infinite
claims which He has upon our love. Nothing is more calculated to cherish and
stir up His love in our hearts than such
discourses, by which we may perhaps be
more enkindled than we might be by
prayer. And really, it is a pitiable thing

sion of piety talk of a thousand needless topics and frivolous reports, of trifles and follies, while we scarcely ever find them speaking of God, or making the Sacred Person of our Lord Jesus Christ the subject of conversation. When we love any one passionately, we have the greatest difficulty in preventing ourselves from speaking of him. Would it not be the same with regard to our Lord if we loved Him, or even if we sincerely desired to love Him? We should also do our utmost, according to our state and condition, by our conversation, our prayers, and many little contrivances which active charity will suggest, to attract every one to this holy love.

MEANS VI.

TO INVOKE THOSE SAINTS WHO HAVE SPECIALLY LOVED OUR LORD.

THE sixth means is to have a special devotion to those Saints who were brought

Person of our Lord, such as the Blessed Virgin, St. Joseph, St. Anne, St. Joachim, and St. John Baptist ; or to such as loved Him with a specially tender and glowing love, as St. Peter, St. John the Evangelist, and St. Mary Magdalen. We should often invoke them, and pray to them to obtain for us a little of that love with which they were so ardently inflamed. Their Feasts should be kept with a particular devotion. I know indeed of some who have composed special litanies to these Saints, in order to beg from them a daily increase of this love.

They can be composed after this manner:

Most holy Virgin, whose love for thy Son was greater than the love of all creatures united, obtain for me His holy love.

St. Joseph, who didst show more love to Jesus than any other man, as thou didst render to Him more services than all others, obtain for me His holy love.

St. John the Baptist, who wast the first to make Jesus known and loved, obtain for me His holy love.

declare thy love for thy Divine Master, obtain for me His holy love.

St. John, who didst draw from the Heart of Jesus, on Which thou didst repose, the flames of that charity with which thou didst burn so intensely, obtain for me His holy love.

St. Mary Magdalen, who, according to the declaration of thy Divine Master, hadst loved Him much, obtain for me His holy love.

It is easy to follow out this plan with regard to other Saints.

MEANS VII.

THE USE OF EJACULATORY PRAYERS.

THE frequent practice of ejaculatory prayer has, at all times, been strongly recommended by the masters of the spiritual life. It was practised by all the Saints, and is still made use of by those who wish

aspire to that union with God which is the
object of this practice. We may say also
that it is especially useful in exciting the
love of Jesus in us, and is one of the best
means of making great progress in it in
a short time.

These ejaculatory prayers are, at one and
the same time, the most effectual causes,
the most ordinary results, and the most
palpable proofs of our love for Jesus. For
some, they are as sparks which rekindle
the heat of an expiring fire ; for others,
the fuel which serves to feed it. In
regard of others, they are as the vehement
blast which puts life into it—the sighs
of the heart wounded with love which tries
to give it vent ; or at least, the interior
sighing of a soul which loves, but does not
love in proportion to its desires, and which
mourns at not loving Jesus sufficiently.
They are aspirations, which are to the
soul what respiration is to the body, vivify-
ing and refreshing it. They are like darts
discharged from a burning heart, which go,

and return from It more ardent and capable
of inflaming the heart from which they
proceed.   They are like so many links
forming an invisible chain, which joins
Heaven to earth, uniting the creature to
God, and God to the creature.   It is thus
that David acquired that wonderful union
with God of which we have such striking
proofs in all the Psalms.   And he declares
that his respirations were not more frequent
than his aspirations to God.*

It seems useless to attempt to teach the
manner of making these ejaculatory prayers
or to give examples of them, since it is
not art but love which should teach us.
It is not the brilliancy of an enlightened
mind, but the fervour of a tender heart
which should form them.   Nevertheless, to
assist beginners, and to make the practice
of it easier to them, we will here suggest
a few of those most likely to excite us
to the love of our Lord Jesus Christ, and
which have been taken from Scripture, or
from the writings of the Saints.

* P. ....::: ...

"I will rejoice in the Lord : and I will joy in God my Jesus."*

"For what have I in Heaven? and besides Thee what do I desire upon earth? Thou art the God of my heart, and the God that is my portion for ever."†

"But God forbid that I should glory, save in the Cross of our Lord Jesus Christ."‡

"For I judged not myself to know any thing among you, but Jesus Christ; and Him crucified."§

"I have suffered the loss of all things, that I may gain Christ."‖

"Who shall separate us from the love of Christ? Shall tribulation? or distress? or famine? or nakedness? or danger? or persecution? or the sword?"¶

"Having a desire to be dissolved and to be with Christ."**

"For to me, to live is Christ : and to die is gain."††

* Hab. iii. 18.
† Ps. lxxii. 25, 26.
‡ Gal. vi. 14.
§ 1 Cor. ii. 2.
‖ Phil. iii. 8.
¶ Rom. viii. 35.
** Phil. i. 23.
†† Phil. i. 21.

"And I live, now not I; but Christ
liveth in me."*

"With Christ I am nailed to the Cross."†

"I love Thee, O Lord, but because I do
not love Thee enough, make me love Thee
more" (St. Augustine).

"Ah! Beauty ever ancient and ever new,
how late have I begun to love Thee!" (St.
Augustine).

"O Holy Fire, Who dost ever burn and
art never extinguished, consume me" (St.
Augustine).

"Thou dost command me, O Lord, to
love Thee; give me grace to do what Thou
commandest, and then command me whatever Thou wilt" (St. Augustine).

"My God and my All" (St. Francis).

* Gal. ii. 20.   † Gal. ii. 19.

MEANS VIII.

TO JOIN AN ASSOCIATION FORMED FOR THE
PURPOSE OF ASKING OF THE ETERNAL FATHER
THE LOVE OF HIS SON, AND CONFORMITY OF
HEART WITH HIM.

I.—What is the design and aim of this Association.

THE eighth and last means is to join an
Association formed for the purpose of
begging constantly the Eternal Father to
produce and increase in us the knowledge
and love of His Only Son, our Lord Jesus
Christ, and conformity of heart with Him,
first, in the hearts of those who belong
to this Association ; secondly, in the hearts
of all the just ; and lastly, in the hearts
of all sinners and unbelievers.   It was
St. Teresa, so full of love towards Jesus
Christ, who being deeply affected by man's
indifference to Jesus Christ, and seeing
Him so little known, or honoured, or loved,
was the first to form and propose this
design.   As she however was not able to
carry it out, two great servants of God,
Father Gaudier and Father Saint Jure,

were inspired a few years ago to put it
in practice, and give it shape. But as it
was only sketched out, I hoped to con-
tribute something to the glory of Jesus
Christ, to the consolation of those who
are desirous of loving Him, and to the
edification of the faithful, if I were to put
the last touch to the execution of so great
and beautiful a design. This I did some
years ago, when I published a book entitled
*Association for entreating the Love of
our Lord*, obtaining at the same time a
Bull of Innocent XI., of happy memory,
which confirmed this Association, and
granted it some Indulgences, that may be
found at the end of the book.

In that book I gave a few exercises,
together with some general and particular
rules for the Association ; and as they may
assist towards the increase of the love of
our Lord Jesus Christ in the hearts of the
Faithful, I have considered it advisable to
place them here.

(1.) Those who have a true desire of acquiring the knowledge and love of Jesus Christ, and who wish to join the Association, need not go through any ceremony for the purpose. It is sufficient to have the intention of devoting themselves to it, and uniting themselves in heart and mind with those who already belong to it.

(2.) After having decided upon this, they must choose a day of Communion for consecrating themselves, by a special devotion, to the Sacred Person of our Lord Jesus Christ. The best time for this act will be immediately after having received the Body of our Lord, when, prostrating themselves in spirit at His Feet with sentiments of lively faith, deep humility, and tender and reverent love, and uniting themselves in heart and mind with all those who belong to the holy Association, with the Saints on Earth and in Purgatory, and with the Blessed in Heaven, they should use the Form which will be found after these rules, for the entire consecration of themselves to the love of Jesus Christ.

(3.) After this, each day during the ensuing week they should take for the subject of their meditation one of the Motives for loving our Lord, so that they may learn to know Jesus Christ, and the infinite obligations we are under to Him, and may have a strong desire of sincerely and ardently loving Him.

CONSECRATION OF THE HEART TO THE LOVE OF JESUS.

O JESUS, Only Son of God, my God, my Creator, and my Saviour, I prostrate myself at Thy Feet with sentiments of the humblest and tenderest gratitude of which a creature is capable, in the presence of the Holy Trinity, of Thy Blessed Mother, of my Guardian Angel, and of all those Saints who were brought into an especial relation with Thee, or had a special love for Thee ; that I may offer homage to Thy Sovereign Majesty, fulfil my duty, and acknowledge my infinite obligations to

Thee. I offer and consecrate myself to
Thee by a special devotion, that I may
apply myself solely to know, love, and
imitate Thee, that henceforth Thou mayest
be the God of my heart, my Love, and
my All ; that I may love none but Thee ;
desire none but Thee ; seek none but Thee;
and live and die but in Thee and for Thee ;
that I may be all Thine, and Thou everything to me; that Thou mayest be my
Possession, my Life, my Repose, my Joy,
my Glory, and my sole and sovereign
Happiness. To this end, I unite myself
in a holy alliance with all the souls whom I
believe to have the same intention of loving
Thee alone, in whatever part of the earth
they may be, and I also unite myself with
the Blessed who are in Heaven, in order
that I may join with them in exercising
this holy love, and in doing my utmost,
in every way I can, to increase it in all
hearts. So that, being united on earth by
the bond of Thy Divine Love, this same
love may one day unite us in Heaven,
there to possess Thee, to praise Thee, to

bless Thee, and to love Thee for ever and
ever.   Amen.

*III.—General Rules by which the Associates should
form their conduct.*

(1.) After having thus devoted and consecrated themselves to the Sacred Person
of our Lord Jesus Christ, they should consider themselves in future as changed men,
as new men, men who no longer are their
own, but Jesus Christ's, to Whom they are
entirely consecrated : " You are not your
own,"* as St. Paul says.   So that all their
talents should be employed solely for Him.
He should be the Beginning and End of
all their emotions and desires, of which
they cannot apply the smallest to the use
of creatures, without an act of robbery,
without a kind of sacrilege ; so that, as
St. Paul says—" They also who live, nay
not now live to themselves, but unto Him
Who died for them."†

(2.) In order that the Associates may
live for Jesus Christ and be animated by

* 1 Cor. vi. 19.   † 2 Cor. v. 15.

His Spirit, they should constantly strive
to destroy in themselves the spirit of the
world, that spirit which is so contrary to
the Spirit of Jesus Christ. They should
accustom themselves to look on the world
as their greatest enemy, because it is the
enemy of Jesus Christ. They ought, then,
to impress well on their minds, that when
once they have pledged themselves to the
Association, and have once decided to
belong to Jesus Christ, they must endeavour
to renounce the world, despise its favours,
hate its ‹maxims, and detest its ways.
They must be fully convinced that they
can have no attachment to it, without
being cowardly deserters, and making themselves guilty of the darkest perfidy.

(3.) It is not enough to endeavour to
renounce and to die to the world: they must
also endeavour to die continually to themselves, to their likings, their passions, their
unruly desires, and to all human move-
ments and natural inclinations, that by these
means they may aspire to that state which
St. Paul reached when He said it was no

longer he, but Jesus Christ Who lived in
him.   To this end they should often have
in their hearts and on their lips that
ejaculatory prayer of a Saint—" My Jesus,
let me die completely to myself, that I
may live only for Thee !"

(4.) To assist themselves to real success
in this great design, the Associates should
apply themselves to the study and knowledge of Jesus Christ, as being their principal, or rather their only, occupation. They
should be constantly thinking of Him,
always contemplating the Greatness and the
Infinite Perfections of this God-Man. They
should diligently meditate His Words, His
Maxims, His Mysteries, His Virtues, His
Actions, and His Example.   They should
have constantly before their eyes, His
Merits, His Benefits, His Kindnesses, and
all the infinite obligations He has laid
upon us ; and especially · they must take
care not only to attend to the exterior, but
also endeavour to enter into the interior
Spirit of Jesus Christ, and the great motives
which influenced Him.   Let these things

be the most ordinary subjects for the reading, meditations, discourses, and ejaculatory prayers of the Associates; for, by being often meditated upon and thoroughly penetrated, they will give a grand conception and a high estimation of the Sacred Person of our Lord Jesus Christ, and of all that appertains to Him. This high estimation will give birth to a solid, enlightened, and constant love. This love will naturally produce a great desire of imitating Jesus Christ, and of putting on Jesus Christ, as the Apostle says; from this desire will grow an entire conformity of heart and mind with Him; and this conformity will infallibly effect that intimate union with Jesus Christ in which consists the happiness and highest perfection of a Christian.

(5.) The Associates must not be content with loving and knowing Jesus Christ for themselves only. If they love Him sincerely, their love will make them burn with a great zeal that He may be known and loved by others. Preachers should endeavour to do this by their sermons;

Directors, by their guidance; others, by their conversation; and those who have not the talent to assist in this way, may help by their prayers. And above all, they must try to induce all those to join the Association, who they think are likely to profit by it: such, for example, as are not infatuated with the spirit of the world, otherwise they would not be suited to the Association, unless indeed they have a sincere desire to strive to detach themselves from the world.

(6.) All the Associates should if possible wear a Crucifix, and strengthen themselves by the sight of it against outbreaks of temper and passion, against the allurements of pleasure, occasions of sin, the vain suggestions of the world, and the temptations of the flesh and the devil. Sometimes they will look on it with love; at others, press it tenderly to their hearts, especially when they feel their heart inclined to give way to some undisciplined emotion; at others they will reverently and tenderly kiss it. Above all, they must never let a day pass without making some little sacrifice for Him Whom it represents.

(7.) All the Associates must have a great charity for one another, must assist each other in their needs, console each other in their afflictions, pray to God often for one another, and stimulate each other by frequent conversations on the love of Jesus Christ ; imitating the Seraphim of the Mercy Seat, who animate and excite one another by the beating of their wings. They must not forget in their prayers the holy souls in Purgatory, who long so ardently to see Jesus Christ. When they hear of the death of an Associate they should assist him by their prayers. Lastly, they must consider themselves as brothers and sisters united in the Heart of Jesus Christ, Who is the Centre of Divine Love, and of this Association.

Neither these rules nor those which follow bind under pain of sin. Nevertheless, it may be said that progress in the love of our Lord Jesus Christ depends very are kept, and the fidelity with which these means are practised.   " Whosoever shall follow this rule, peace be on them."*

IV.—What is to be done every day.

(1.) At our morning prayer we must ask the Eternal Father to plant or increase in our hearts, and in the hearts of the Associates, and of all mankind, Christians or unbelievers, just or unjust, the knowledge and love of His Son Jesus Christ our Saviour, and conformity of heart and mind with Him.

(2.) The same prayer should be made at Mass, at the Elevation, and at the time of Holy Communion, whether Spiritual or Sacramental ; and again before going to bed at night, after our examination of conscience.   The following prayer can be used for the purpose.

PRAYER FOR OBTAINING HOLY LOVE, TO BE SAID DAILY BY THE ASSOCIATES FOR ONE ANOTHER.

(1.) O JESUS, the Only Son of God and our Sovereign Lord, Who by an infinite

excess of goodness and love hast been
pleased to clothe Thyself with our flesh
and make Thyself like unto us in all things,
that Thou mightest show forth in us the
riches of Thy Grace and of Thy Glory ;
we earnestly beseech Thee, for ourselves
and for those united to us in a special
bond for the purpose of loving and imitating
Thee, to vouchsafe us the favour of uniting
Thyself to us by the inseparable bond of
Thy Divine Charity, and by a perfect conformity of our hearts and minds to Thee.
To this end destroy in us the spirit of the
world, and replenish us with Thy Holy
Spirit, that He may make us live by Thy
Divine Life, that being dead to ourselves we
may live only to Thee, O Lord, who didst
condescend to die for us; and that we may
all together acknowledge Thee eternally as
our Redeemer, praise and honour Thee as
our Sovereign Lord, adore and love Thee
as our God : Who livest and reignest, with
the Father and the Holy Ghost, world without end.   Amen.

(2.) The Litany of the Holy Name of

Jesus is to be said for the same intention. Those who cannot read, instead of the Litany of the Holy Name, may say five Our Fathers and five Hail Marys in honour of the Five Wounds of our Lord.

(3.) No day should pass without our doing, for this intention, some good work or act of mortification either interior or exterior. We must endeavour to perform our actions in a spirit of union with those of Jesus Christ, looking on Him, not simply as the only object of our love, but also as the only Model upon which we are to form ourselves. So that each of our actions may be, as it were, another touch which we add to finish this Divine Likeness in us.

(4.) Those who have more leisure, and are masters of their time and occupations, can profitably make use of an exercise which some holy persons have adopted for obtaining the love of our Lord Jesus Christ, and from which they have derived great fruit. It is to make daily three visits to the Blessed Sacrament, in honour of the Most Holy Trinity, to ask of each Person the perfection of this holy love. To assist such as desire to practise this, we here add three prayers to the Three Persons of the Blessed Trinity asking for this holy love. They will be the more efficacious before God and likely to strengthen our confidence, in as much as they are almost entirely taken from Scripture, especially from the Gospel of St. John and the Epistles of St. Paul.

PRAYER TO THE ETERNAL FATHER TO ASK FOR LOVE OF HIS SON.

Almighty and Eternal God, Father of our Lord Jesus Christ, with the same sentiments of love and gratitude with which I thank Thee for having so loved the world as to give us Thy Son, through Whom we may have access to Thee, I now beseech Thee to accomplish the promise Thou didst make to Him, of giving Him all nations for an inheritance, and to reward Him for the sacrifice He made to Thee of His Life and His Blood by giving Him a numerous posterity. Draw us then to Him, O Lord, by the power of Thy grace ;

glorify Him in us, as He has glorified Thee
in Himself. Grant that our Divine Saviour
may live always in our hearts by lively
faith, sincere charity, and the perfect conformity of our hearts and minds to Him.
Strengthen and enlighten the eyes of our
mind that we may fully understand how
lofty are the hopes of His vocation in us,
what are the riches of His glory which
He has prepared for His Saints, and what
the extent of the force and greatness of
His might, that so we may love Him as
Thou hast loved Him, and that as Thou
hast put everything in subjection to His
Power, so also there may be nothing in us
which is not wholly consecrated and perfectly subjected to Him, as our God, as
our King, as our Head, and that He may
reign over us in Time and in Eternity.

PRAYER TO THE SON TO BEG OF HIM HIS HOLY LOVE.

O most lovely and adorable Jesus, my
God and my Saviour, from Whom proceed
all the blessings I have or that I hope
to have; Thou Who art the Light of the

World, the Only and Infallible Way which
leads to Thy Father, the Truth which
saves us from lies and delivers us from
error, the Gate, by which he who enters
shall be saved, the Source of Life, Who
hast made known to the world that life
of heavenly love, which was hidden from
all Eternity in the Bosom of Thy Father,
by making to shine forth in Thyself all the
riches of the Goodness and Mercy of God,
till then unknown to mankind : accomplish
Thy Joy in us, as Thou hast promised, by
making us and all men serve to the ad-
vancement of Thy Glory and the increase
of Thy Holy Love. Shed on us, to this
end, that Heavenly Light, which Thou
camest to bring on earth, that the love
which Thy Father hath for Thee may be
in us, as Thou, by Thy Holy Word, hast
made us to hope ; and, as He is in Thee,
as He is but One with Thee, so may we
be but one with Thee by a perfect conformity of life and manners ; so that we
may have nothing in us which is not wholly
subject and entirely devoted to Thee, and

being dead to the world, the flesh, and our--
selves by an entire renouncement of all
but Thee, we may henceforth live for Thee,
Who livest and reignest for ever and ever.
Amen.

PRAYER TO THE HOLY GHOST TO BEG OF HIM THE
LOVE OF OUR LORD JESUS CHRIST.

O Holy Ghost, All powerful God, Eternal
Love of the Adorable Trinity, Sacred Fire
that unitest the Father with the Son, Who
proceeding from them both, hast also been
sent by both into the world to glorify
Jesus Christ and to give testimony of Him,
so that no one can know Him without
Thee, nor pronounce the Name of Jesus,
as they ought, without Thy aid: we beseech Thee to accomplish in us this great
design, for which Thou wast sent, by giving
this testimony to us in heart and spirit,
the witness that Jesus Christ is our God,
our Master, and our Saviour, the Way, the
Truth, and the Life, that He came to
reveal to us in Time those ineffable mysteries hidden from all Eternity in the

Bosom of the Father, and to communicate
to us all the treasures of the Divinity,
which till then He had retained in Himself.
Pour down on us Thy Heavenly Unction
to sweeten the seeming hardships of His
holy yoke, that we may take delight in
His maxims, understand His mysteries,
follow faithfully His guidance, enter into
the designs of His wisdom and of His
mercy to us ; lastly, that we may attach
ourselves to Him solely and constantly by
that sincere and generous love which Thou
alone canst produce in our hearts.

It is Thine, O Holy Spirit, to make us
ask this favour by those secret and ineffable groanings of which Thou art the
author ; and it is Thine also to grant it us,
for Thou art the Author of all gifts, that
as it is by Thee that the Father is united
to the Son and the Son to the Father, so
also it may be by Thee that He is united
to us and we to him for ever and ever.
Amen.

V.—*What is to be done every Month.*

(1.) A fixed day should be chosen in each Month, when the Associates are to communicate for this intention, and beg the Eternal Father with redoubled fervour for the increase of knowledge and love of His Son, and conformity of heart and mind with Him.

(2.) When they have received the Body of our Lord, they should prostrate themselves in spirit at His Feet, and renew the consecration by which they bound themselves to the Association.

(3.) On this day they should spend half an hour, or at least a quarter of an hour, before the Blessed Sacrament, partly to pray for the increase of this love, partly to meditate on the Greatness and Perfection of our Lord Jesus Christ, the obligations under which we lie to Him, and the mysteries of His Life and Death.

(4.) They should endeavour on this day to read some book which treats of the love or imitation of our Lord Jesus Christ.

(5.) If they can do it conveniently, they should also endeavour to pay a visit to some poor persons ashamed to appear so, or to prisoners, or to sick persons, in order thus to do honour to Jesus Christ in His members.

VI.—*What is to be done every Year.*

(1.) Two Feasts should be chosen for the more solemn renewal of the Consecration by which we are bound to the pious Association. These should be, that of the Nativity of our Lord, and that of His Transfiguration, which the Associates should honour with a special devotion, as being the two Feasts when the Eternal Father made known His Son to the world and to His disciples, and offered Him as the Object of their adoration, their love, and their imitation.

(2.) They must endeavour, on the eves of these two Feasts, to prepare themselves by some mortification or work of mercy, and above all by retirement : giving more on that day, whether in prayer or reading, only with the Greatness and Perfection of the Word Incarnate, the infinite obligations we owe Him, and the special promise we have made to love Him and imitate Him.

To assist persons in this holy exercise, during the Octave of the Nativity they can take for their meditation the devotions proper for the season, which they will find in the book called *Interior Exercises.* During the Octave of the Transfiguration the Eight Motives for the Love of Jesus, which form the matter of the First Part of this book, can be used.

USEFUL HINTS FOR THOSE WHO LOVE GOD, AND WHO DESIRE TO GROW IN HIS LOVE.

(1.) You have given and devoted yourself to God in all the fulness of your heart: never cease to ratify this offering. Consecrate to Him continually all your thoughts, all your affections, and all your actions. Often tell Him that you wish your mind to be occupied with Him alone, and with

those things which He wills you to think
of ; that you wish your heart to love none
but Him, and your brethren only in Him,
according to the rule of charity ; that you
wish all you do and all you suffer to be
offered to him ; that you wish the end
of your actions to be His glory and good
pleasure. Tell Him that you rejoice at
being no longer your own but His, that
you will never cease to place your liberty
in His Hands, to direct it, and to do what
He wills with it.

Give yourself unreservedly to God, the
Author and Preserver of your being, Who
has done you nothing but good, and Who
desires to make you eternally happy. You
have only the present moment at your
disposal. It is only in giving yourself
entirely to God that you can glorify Him,
sanctify yourself, and fulfil as He requires
the great precept of loving Him. The
example of Jesus Christ makes this
complete and irrevocable offering a law
for you. In this gift of yourself to God
consists that renunciation which is com-

manded in the Gospel. It is by this that
you really merit the title of child of God,
and have a moral certainty of your salvation ; it is by this that you dry up the spring
of the reproaches of conscience ; it is by
this that you obtain peace of soul, the
gift of prayer, and a great familiarity with
God ; and it is by this that you will enter
into the way of holiness.

Give yourself to God with all the love
of which you are capable during the short
time you are in this life. He intends to
give Himself to you with an infinite love
for eternity.

(2.) Serve Jesus through love. Let love
guide you in everything. Let love be
your only spring of action. Fear is the
beginning of wisdom ; you ought to fear,
but let your fear be a filial fear. Fear to
displease God because He is your Father.
Hope is a virtue ; you ought to hope.
Desire and confidently expect to receive
Heaven from the goodness of God, through
the merits of your Saviour, and thus to
be forced certainly and necessarily to love

God with all your strength through all eternity.

He who serves God through love sees God everywhere, and He sees Him everywhere only to love Him. It is especially by this practice that we glorify and please God, that we are more quickly and thoroughly purified, that we make ourselves worthy of the favours of the Almighty, and that we heap up rich treasures in Heaven.

How sweet it is to serve God through love! He who serves Him thus, dearly loves the will of God, and desires to know it that He may fulfil it, and when he knows it he executes it with promptitude. He is tenderly loved by God, Who is Peace, and so he possesses peace which passeth all understanding. His heart is filled with a pure, deep, unchangeable joy, a joy which is a foretaste of that which inundates the souls of the Blessed.

To serve God through love is not difficult. He gave us a heart, that we might love Him. and He alone is infinitely loveable.

If, with the intention of pleasing Him, and by the constant consideration of His amiable qualities you excite yourself to a pure love of Him, will He refuse you when you ask earnestly for the graces you require for His service ?

(3.) Order leads to God.   He who faithfully observes for the love of God a good rule of life, in a manner that pleases Him, will daily advance in His knowledge and love.   Here follows a kind of rule of life, the observing of which may be very useful to you.

Have a fixed time for rising, for meals, religious exercises, employments, and for repose.   Never alter these unless necessity or charity demand it.

Do all for the greater glory of God.

Never conform yourself to the world. You must look on it as the enemy of Jesus Christ and your enemy.   Do not make friendship with those who allow themselves to be dazzled by its vanities, and who follow its false pleasures.

PRAYERS.

ACT OF REPARATION TO THE SACRED HEART OF JESUS.

O ADORABLE Heart of my Saviour and my God! penetrated with a lively sorrow at the sight of the insults which Thou hast received, and still dost daily receive, in the Sacrament of the Eucharist, I here prostrate myself to make reparation to Thee at the foot of Thy Altar. Oh! that I might by my homage and devotion make amends to Thee for Thy neglected Majesty! Oh! that I might efface by my tears and my blood all the numberless acts of irreverence, profanation, and sacrilege! How well my life would be spent if I might give it for such an object! Grant the pardon which I beg of Thee, O my God, for all the numberless heretics who dishonour Thee. Pardon me, too, especially, who have so often insulted Thee. Remember that in carrying the weight of my sins Thy Adorable Heart was afflicted even unto death. Permit not that Thy sufferings and Thy Blood should be profitless to me. Destroy my heart of wickedness and give me one like Thine, a contrite humble heart, a pure and spotless heart, a heart which for the future shall be nothing but a victim devoted to Thy glory, and burning with the Sacred Fire of Thy Love. On my part I promise that by the modesty of my behaviour in church, by my assiduity in visiting Thee, by my devotion and fervour in receiving Thee, to make reparation for all the irreverences and sacrileges which I deplore in the bitterness of my heart. To make my adoration and devotion more pleasing to Thee, I unite them to those of the Angels and the Blessed Spirits who are prostrate at the foot of Thy Tabernacles, and who weep bitterly in Thy Presence. Hear our prayers, O my God! and reject not a sinner who returns to Thee with the desire of being all Thine for ever. Amen.

PRAYER TO THE SACRED HEART OF MARY.

O SACRED Heart of Mary! ever Virgin, and Immaculate in thy most holy Conception, Heart the holiest, the purest, the most perfect, the most noble, the greatest which the Hand of the Almighty Creator has ever formed in a pure creature, Heart the unfailing source of grace, of goodness, of sweetness, of mercy, and of love, model of all virtues, perfect likeness of the Adorable Heart of Jesus Christ, Heart ever on fire with the most ardent charity; who by thyself hast loved God more than the Seraphim, more than all the Angels and Saints united, who hast given more glory to the Blessed Trinity by the least of thy actions than has been given or could have been given by all other creatures by the most heroic of theirs, Heart of the Mother of our Redeemer, who hast felt so keenly our miseries, who hast suffered so much for our salvation, who hast loved us so ardently and tenderly, and who dost merit in every possible way the love and veneration, the gratitude and confidence of all mankind, deign to receive my feeble homage and devotion.

Prostrate before thee, O Sacred Heart of the Mother of Mercy, I offer thee the profoundest homage due to thee. I thank thee for all the mercy and love with which thou hast been and still art touched at the sight of my misery. I thank thee for all the favours which I have received from thy motherly goodness. I unite myself to all those pure souls who find their delight and consolation in honouring, praising, and loving thee ; for they have learnt from the Holy Spirit, Who guides them, that it is through thee that we must go to Jesus Christ, and through thee that we are to pay this Man-God all the service that we owe to Him.

Thou then, O Heart worthy of all love ! thou shalt be, after the Heart of thy dear and Divine Son, the object of my veneration, my love, and my most tender devotion. Thou shalt be the way by which I approach my Saviour, and by Thee I shall receive

His graces and mercies. Thou shalt be
my Refuge in my afflictions, my Consolation in my troubles, my Help in all my
needs. I will come to thee to learn Purity,
Humility, Sweetness, and especially Love
of the Sacred Heart of Jesus Christ thy
Son. I will ask these virtues through thy
merits; and thus I hope to obtain them,
and, with them, the pardon of my sins, '
and the gift of final perseverance. Amen.

www.ingramcontent.com/pod-product-compliance
Lightning Source LLC
Chambersburg PA
CBHW020800020726
47495CB00008B/2519